How to Ruin
a Perfectly
Good Relationship

Published by
Zeig, Tucker & Theisen, Inc.
3614 North 24th Street
Phoenix, AZ 85016

Library of Congress Cataloging-in-Publication Data
Love, Patricia.
    How to ruin a perfectly good relationship / by Pat Love & Sunny
Shulkin. — Rev. ed.
    p. cm.
    ISBN 10: 1-891944-88-6 / ISBN 13: 978-1-891944-88-8
    1. Man–woman relationships. I. Shulkin, Sunny. II. Title.
    HQ801.L67 2003
    306.7—dc21   2003045025

Manufactured in the United States of America

10 9 8 7 6 5 4 3 2

How to Ruin a Perfectly Good Relationship

Revised Edition

By

Pat Love, EdD

& Sunny Shulkin, LCSW

Zeig, Tucker & Theisen, Inc.
Phoenix, Arizona

Prologue
from Sunny and Pat

On the way to learning how to make a relationship work, some of us have to "explore" what can go wrong first. Between the two of us, we have done a lot of exploration, making a lot of the mistakes presented in this little book. And we have made some of them many times. So we know what we are talking about, and we bet you do too if you can step back just a bit and judge your behavior objectively.

We hope to make you laugh a little ... and more important, we hope that that laugh leads to an attempt to change some of your following habits. Seriously, research indicates that the preceding behaviors – no matter how insignificant they seem – over time erode the love between two people. The most common reason couples offer for separation is that they have "grown apart." We will show you some of what growing apart actually looks like along the way.

If you catch it now, you can do something positive about it.

Be late. Often.

No need to say a word,
your partner will know
whose time is more important.

If there's a problem,

sweep it under the rug.
Wait until it's too late to seek help.

Withhold sex. ♂

♀ Extra points for this one.

Be stingy

with praise.

Withhold information.

Let important news reach
your partner via other means,
like your mother or secretary.

Give ample time and attention

to everyone but your partner.
("Isn't the waiter charming?")

Don't ask ... don't tell

... about sexual needs.

Wait as long as possible

to respond to your
partner's complaints.

Don't give in ... ever!

(Unless, of course, you hear something like,
"I've had it, I'm outta here.")

Tell your partner you'll be willing to discuss it when ...

The game is over

The kids are asleep

This work project is done

You've returned a couple of important calls
(or e-mails)

You're back from the gym

You've cleaned out the closets

You've taken some time to unwind

In the morning

Tell your partner you'll be ready for sex when ...

The game is over

The kids are asleep

This work project is done

You've returned a couple of important calls
(or e-mails)

You're back from the gym

You've cleaned out the closets

You've taken some time to unwind

In the morning

Keep on the move

when your partner is trying
to talk to you

Channel surf

when your partner wants
to discuss something

If what your partner says

makes you uncomfortable,
dismiss it with "You're nuts."

Come home late and be sure to have an arsenal of responses:

"Why are you always on my case?"

"Somebody's gotta pay for all this."

"Who put you in charge?"

"Can't I have a minute to myself?"

"What exactly are you implying?"

"The battery died on my cell."

"Sometimes I need to talk to a friend, okay?"

"Get off my back, will ya."

Refuse professional help when you need it:

"I know more about me
than any therapist!"

"Those guys are crazier
than their patients."

"I don't need some jerk
poking around in my private life."

"It's pouring money down the drain."

"You're the one who needs a shrink!"

Let disagreements fester.

Shut out your partner.

See all problems as signs
that the relationship will not work.

Say what you think your
partner wants to hear,
and then do as you please.

Always be planning your exit strategy.

Walk out

in the middle of arguments.

Leave your partner's side

as soon as you get to the party.

Wander away in public places

so your partner has to look for you.

Be defensive
when ...

Your partner requests
even the slightest change in behavior

Your partner disagrees with you

Your partner asks for information

You feel insecure

You want to assert your authority

In public be charming, in private be ...

Silent

Critical

Unresponsive

Sarcastic

Holier than thou

Whiney

Belittling

See yourself as better

than your partner

See yourself as better

than your partner's friends
or family

Make sure that your interactions

with your partner are at least
80% negative

When you have a problem

with your partner (or with anything)
mums the word,
just add it to your list of resentments

Be nice to everyone

but your partner (remember the waiter)

If you find you happen to be enjoying something,

quickly focus on an unhappy time and
get back to your old self

Keep score.

When you have an argument,
you should have a list of things
your partner did wrong
in the past to use.

Make sure your partner knows

how unhappy you are so that
he or she will feel
guilty and responsible

Make it as hard as possible

for your partner to apologize ...
and then don't accept it

Turn molehills into mountains

every time!

Bad mouth your partner

to your friends.

Bad mouth your partner's friends

to your partner.

Express disappointment

every chance you get.

If you don't want to talk about something,

divert your partner's attention by
mentioning something else that is
guaranteed to stir up hurt feelings.

Adopt the life motto:

My way or the highway!

Adopt the mantra:

Sulk

Pout

Nag

Sulk

Pout

Nag

Breathe in, breathe out

Mock your partner

in front of others.

Belittle his or her

politics, taste, occupation,
financial skills, cooking ability,
. . . whatever.

A poem:

Blame, blame, blame

Shame, shame, shame,

Complain, complain, complain

Drive recklessly

Be embarrassingly loud

Cut your partner off
in conversation

Grunt your responses

Hold a grudge

Grow
more and more bitter

Never forgive

and

Never forget

When you don't want to have sex,

pick a fight

Exchange any gifts

your partner buys for you

Forget your anniversary

Save your good moods

for other people

Spurn your partner's

attempts to solve problems

Become surprisingly angry over little things,

but when your partner is angry
accuse him or her of being
dramatic and hysterical.

Angrily insist

that you are not angry.

Discourage your partner

from expressing views using patronization,
disdain, or the threat of volatility.

Talk about breaking up.

Blame everything on PMS,

whether yours or your partner's.

Use the children:

to punish your partner

to gang up on your partner

to pity you

to side with you

to protect you

as an excuse

Always be looking around

for potential new mates

Treat your partner like a child

Act like a child

See every opportunity for change

as an excuse to leave

Look down on

your partner's passions

Blame the children's

problems or shortcomings
on your partner

Leave little room for conversation,

even less for affection

Control

everything and everyone

Never
accept responsibility

Point the finger

early and often

Don't stay within your
budget

(even if you insist
that your partner does)

Win every fight,
and don't let up until you do

Keep score

Threaten

Use your partner's vulnerabilities
against him or her

See every discussion

as a precursor to a fight.

Once the fight has started ...

Escalate!

Expect your partner to be able to read your mind:

"If you loved me, you'd know."

Find fault,

especially when your partner
is trying to please you.

Demand fidelity;

refuse sex ♂

♀ Extra points

Drink

Get drunk

Pass out ♂

♀ Extra points

Lie ♂

♀ A little goes a very long way

Use silence

as a weapon

Pretend you don't hear

Think of an apology as an excuse

to bring up additional complaints

Never take your partner's advice

(especially if it makes sense)

If you suddenly realize you are wrong,

back-peddle and insist that you
never said any such thing.

Make promises;

don't keep them

Assign your partner

most of the household chores and then
criticize how they are carried out

Give in
whether or not you mean it,
to avoid confrontation

Withhold real feelings

Spend hours

on the phone or internet

Never ask for help

Never help

Question

your partner's commitment

When your partner needs some time alone,

make sure to interpret it
as a sleight

Confide in friends,

not in your partner

Give advice

when it's not requested

Perfect the art of

"I told you so."

Act as though you are living alone by:

Never picking up after yourself

Only preparing snacks for yourself

Flipping channels
whether or not the other person
is watching something

Taking the last of anything that's in the fridge

Changing décor
without consulting your partner

Making purchases for the house
without looking at the shared budget

Never listening

Never talking

Refuse to seek help

for depression

Refuse

to see depression in your partner

Refuse

to find ways to control anger

Treat the television better

than you do your partner

Don't cultivate friendships,

get grumpy when your partner does

Don't be romantic

Refuse
all gestures of affection

Be proud of
your intimacy issues

Medicate

instead of dealing with problems

Pretend that knowing your problem

is the same as working it out

Use your partner's therapy against him or her:

"What, did your shrink teach you that?"

Use what you learn in therapy

or from self-help books
against your partner

Insist that your partner

had a terrible childhood,
that his or her parents were out to lunch,
and that's why . . .

Pick

on your partner's appearance

Compare your partner

to your friends

Get sulky

if your partner doesn't compliment
fast enough

Withdraw

emotionally

Be secretive

Ambush your partner when

discussing seemingly innocuous subjects;
start a fight

Meticulously analyze your partner's faults;

don't worry about your own

Let lots of time go by

between loving gestures

Show off about other people

being attracted to you

Forget the words

"I love you."

Blame your partner

because you haven't fulfilled your dreams

Don't deal with job-related frustrations

at work when you can bring them home.

Never give your partner the benefit of the doubt

Become well versed in the language

of emotional blackmail

Don't be above using verbal abuse;

it works

Tease

Don't do your part

Don't listen

Take your partner for granted

Complain about money

and then complain about
your partner's working too many hours

Undermine

your partner's parenting decisions

Never give in

Always give in

Always make clear

that leaving the relationship
is a viable option

Be relentless in your demands

Flirt with others

Become emotionally entangled with someone else,

explaining that the
relationship is not "cheating" since
there isn't any (physical) sexual contact

Insist that your partner

express feelings and then become incensed
when he or she does

Take advantage

of your partner's insecurities

Initiate

serious conversions
just as your partner is falling asleep

Ignore

your partner's sexual needs
Also his or her emotional needs

Fail to notice positive changes

in your partner's appearance

Turn away your partner's sexual overtures

Compare your current sexual relationship

to previous ones

Force sex on your partner

Make fun of your partner's attempts

at sexual exploration

Blame your partner

for your own sexual difficulties

Talk crassly about sex

when you know it upsets your partner

Make your partner feel bad

about having a different level (greater or lesser) of sexual drive than you

Only touch your partner

during sex

Recoil at your partner's touch

Refuse to experiment sexually ♂

♀ Extra points for accelerating the beginning of the end

Expect the relationship

to continue without being nurtured

Roll over and go to sleep

Wake your partner up to have sex

without concern for
his or her need for sleep

Never talk about sex

Avoid touching your partner's body

Avoid kissing

Fake orgasm

and become more and more
resentful about it

Don't talk about your physical needs,

but expect your partner to know them anyway

Pretend you are sleeping

when your partner comes to bed

Treat sex as a necessary evil

Use sex to manipulate

Brush your teeth after sex

rather than before

Be a slob

Be rude just before bed

and then expect sex

When your partner opens up about his or her feelings ...

Watch TV out of the corner of your eye

Interpret, analyze, interrupt

Look scared

Explode

Become detached and cold

Discount

Walk out

Getting in the Last Word

As this little book comes to a close, we hope you have found enlightenment, the enlightenment of catching yourself in the act of ruining a perfectly good relationship. It's easier than you thought, isn't it? Who would have known that forgetting to be on time — the way you promised — could scar her soul? Who would have believed that making him the butt of a joke in front of your friends would drive iron nails through his heart? Simply stated, easily overlooked: *it does*. We are so busy feeling hurt by our partners that we don't take the time to stop and look at ourselves — and realize that we are the ones doing the hurting.

Although this book may seem like a lark — don't be fooled. Gently disguised by tongue-in-cheek humor, each page is popping with kernels of wisdom to help you learn the types of behavior that predict unhappy relationships and divorce. So take a few minutes. Take the words seriously. Ask yourself, "Do I really want to ruin this perfectly good relationship?" If you see yourself on almost every page, chances are that is *exactly* what you are doing!

The good news is that it's never too late to confess we've blundered. We've all made more than enough mistakes to fill the Hoover Dam, requiring weeks to bail ourselves out. Forget the excuses and justifications, even when you're right. It's good for the soul — and your relationship — to make amends. Relationships need kindness, generosity, tenderness, and equality. There can be no good relationship without them.

So, if you can't defend or justify or call foul, what can you say or do when you've caught yourself in the act of ruining a perfectly good relationship? Fess up and say, "I've done it again, haven't I? I forgot your feelings. I forgot your needs. I acted alone and didn't give you a chance to vote. Geez, I came mighty close to ruining a perfectly good relationship!" If you think that's nonsense, you just might be absolutely perfect at ruining relationships.

We hope you'll continue to read, and learn from, this simple little book over and over again. We hope you'll share it with your partner. We hope you'll pass it on to your very best friends, and they'll pass it on to their best friends. Let's keep this book circulating until peace and love reign throughout the land, starting in your own backyard.

Bon Voyage.